CW01457592

Copyright © 2019 Yvonne Sonsino

All rights reserved. No part of this publication may be reproduced, stored in a retrieval system or transmitted, in any form or by any means, without the prior written permission of the author, except in accordance with the provisions of the Copyright, Designs and Patents Act 1988.
Any person who undertakes any unauthorised act in relation to this publication may be liable to criminal prosecution and civil claims for damages.

First published 2019
Printed and bound in the UK by Biddles, King's Lynn
ISBN 978-1-913218-68-3

Acknowledgements

We'd like to thank all our tutors and students for their continued support and encouragement without which this book would never have been produced. We'd especially like to thank John Priest for all his patience, hard work and the generous time he's put into the 'behind-the-scenes' activities such as the small job of editing and print layout.

ARDINGTON

Book of Bakes & Preserves

By Yvonne Sonsino & Holly Knight

Published by Ardington School of Crafts

This book is dedicated to Wendy, who never got to see the school, but her memory lives on in the flapjack recipe. Warm and chewy, and slightly crispy round the edges, just as you liked them.

Welcome to the Ardington Book of Bakes & Preserves

Preface

This has been lovingly put together by Yvonne Sonsino, Director of Ardington School, and her daughter Holly Knight, by popular demand. Simply put, our students and tutors keep asking "How do you get those scones so light?! Please share the recipe." "What's in that ginger sponge? It's gorgeous!" "That Ardington Bakewell Tart is to die for". And other lovely comments. So we – in the spirit of shared learning which is what the Ardington philosophy is all about - are sharing our secrets here with you.

First secret:

We have a trained chef in the Ardington School family. Simon is a trained chef, and has always enjoyed preparing great food and enjoying great company. Having spent many years with high street name restaurants and hotels, including the Hilton, he now indulges his creativity in Textual Art and Calligraphy, as well as running the school. It's a seven day a week love affair with the greatest little craft school in Britain.

Second secret:

Yvonne and Holly are keen amateur cooks who love baking and entertaining. They are quite happy baking cakes for four hundred people in a weekend, for National Garden Scheme openings in recent years. And, the family did run their own restaurant for a few years, down in Salisbury. It was hard work, but we are proud of the lovely food we got out in those days, and the great Secret Shopper review we had in The Sunday Times!

Third secret:

There are no calories at Ardington school. Shhhhh….

So we hope you enjoy this collection of good home-baking and go on to share some of our secrets with your own family and friends, just as we have done over the years.

Introduction

It's difficult to pick a favourite cake. The buttermilk scones are an absolute winner and when we produced rhubarb and ginger versions with complementary home-made rhubarb and rose petal jam and whipped cream, they literally went like hotcakes. White chocolate and raspberry cheesecake is also very popular and comes a close second. Lemon drizzle, ginger sponge and chocolate cakes are also ever popular classics.

Some of these recipes are family secrets; for example the dark chocolate sponge cake which Yvonne learned how to make in the Domestic Science lessons at King Edward VI Grammar School for Girls way back in the 1970s. This recipe has to be one of the easiest chocolate cake recipes in the world and it's been passed on from generation to generation, and from friend to friend around the world.

We've also invented our own new cake recipes such as the Ardington Bakewell Tart, which uses home grown, home-made blackcurrant jam and has its own special blackcurrant icing topping. There will be many new recipes added to the collection in the coming years and we look forward to sharing them with you and welcoming you to Ardington to try them for yourself.

A typical food-day at Ardington

The day starts at Ardington with 'Cookie O'Clock' when a batch of cookie dough is shaped, crimped and baked ready for our students arrival at 9.30am. The cookies welcome our students and go nicely with a freshly brewed hot coffee, a selection of teas or a frothy hot chocolate.

We love to make the cookies in different shapes and sizes because, as we know, no one-size fits all. Some cookie munchers like them crispy. Some prefer them soft and chewy. Some like a 'healthy' cookie like oat and flax seed. Others prefer full on fudge and double chocolate. The range of flavours for home-baked cookies seems almost endless, and seasonal varieties creep in at Christmas.

As the morning session closes with the ringing of the school bell, lunch is served on the antique dresser in the dining room. It groans under the weight of the freshly made selection. No sooner has the lunch been cleared away, the afternoon workshop session starts. Then it's time to prepare the afternoon tea.

Afternoon tea is officially 'Cake O'Clock at Ardington' and served by 3pm. This time it is signalled by the ringing of the smaller, more delicate afternoon-tea-size-bell rather than the great big lunch bell that often scares our students, in deep crafting-concentration, witless!

Any spare cake (as if) at the end of the day, will often go home with a tutor for their long-suffering partners.

How this book is structured

In this book, we have included a specially selected range of our favourite cake bake recipes, and where appropriate, the occasional extra goody. We are simple cooks. When you are baking cakes for 150 students and tutors on a weekly basis, you have to keep it simple. You will find many of the methods in here are therefore the 'All-in-One' style – that is, you put all or most of the ingredients into one big bowl at once and use a hand mixer or table top mixer like a Kitchen Aid to mix them. Then you bake them. Simple.

Diets and nutrition are complicated these days, and our visitors have a range of likes, dislikes and allergies. Where we can adapt a recipe to be gluten free, or dairy free, we do, and details of those we adapt are included on each of the recipe pages in this book.

We have deliberately included Imperial and Metric measurements in each recipe, because we still speak both languages. We have also included baking instructions for electric, gas and Aga owners. Most of our baking is now done in the Aga, which means as any Aga owner out there will know, there's a little mystery involved as far as timing and temperature are concerned. Keep's it interesting! Fan ovens can also be a bit fierce, so we offer a fan oven suggested temperature in each case too.

One other important thing to note is that we bake at scale. We don't make a batch of six fairy cakes at a time. Usually the smallest batch of anything we make feeds at least 16. If the recipe is too large for you, then we have a number of suggestions:

- Freeze the surplus – all of our cake recipes freeze really well
- Halve the recipe quantities
- Eat more
- Share some with friends, relatives and neighbours. You may enjoy a whole new social life as a result!

We have added Top Tips wherever we can, because in some cases, it is possible to improve upon the basics. These tips include ways to change the core recipe into a new cake or cookie. You will find that you are chopping and changing flavours and ingredients in no time, once you have experimented a little.

So there is no need to buy another baking book ever! This is part of the shared learning process of this book – giving you permission to experiment and create new things. Just like doing a craft course, you can go home and try it yourself on the kitchen table!

All spoon measurements are level spoons, unless stated.

homemade
Rhubarb
&
Ginger
Scones

Cream
Tea
REMEMBER: JAM FIRST, THEN CREAM

homemade
&
home grown
Rhubarb
&
Rose Petal
Jam

THE ARLINGTON
"BAKEWELL"

WHITE CHOC
& MACADAMIA
COOKIES

Bakes

Preserves

Bakes

Ardington Cookies

Makes 2 x rolls of 8 to 10 cookies

① 125g (5oz) butter, softened and diced (use a vegetable spread to make dairy free)

② 250g (9oz) light brown sugar

③ 225g (8oz) self–raising flour

④ 1 teaspoon vanilla extract or 1 rounded tablespoon custard powder

⑤ 1 free-range egg, lightly beaten

⑥ Optional Extras: 100g (4oz) chocolate chips or pieces or 100g (4oz) granola or rounded tablespoon flax seed or 2 rounded tablespoons peanut butter or 1 rounded tablespoon chopped Macadamia Nuts, or 1 rounded tablespoon Dried Cranberries, or 100g (4oz) granola

or any combination of these or your own favourite extras.

For a cocoa cookie, add 40g of cocoa powder to your flour at the start.

The beauty of this recipe is that it is really simple to make and to change up. You can stick to the same basic ingredients for the cookie dough but you can add such a wide variety of different extras, it means you can have different flavours every time you make them. These cookies are buttery, crispy round the edges, chewy in the middle and sweet. Also, they are so handy to have as ready-to-bake cookie dough in the freezer, as they bake perfectly with a short defrost. In fact, if the dough is super cold when you shape it ready for baking, then your cookies will keep a good shape and look great when baked.

Top tip ~ for baking, roll each cookie into a ball and flatten with a potato masher dipped in flour to around 1 cm thick. It makes a rugged imprint and the cookies look really authentic!

Method

Pre-heat oven to 180°C, Gas mark 6, Aga baking oven on middle runners

Place items 1 to 5 (and cocoa if using) in a large bowl and mix with a hand mixer for about one minute until blended well. Add the beaten egg slowly as you continue mixing. A cookie dough will form. Add your choice of extra flavouring from item 6 and mix lightly until combined. Turn onto a floured board and knead lightly. Cut in half. Form into two rolls, (like a Swiss roll shape) and each makes about 8 to 10 cookies. Chill or freeze until ready to bake and then cut into 1 cm slices ready for baking. As per top tip, roll each piece into a ball and flatten with a potato masher for an authentic looking cookie.

Bake on a tray: 10 to 12 minutes

Ardington Buttermilk Scones

Makes 2 batches of 8 to 10 scones

1. 450g (1lb) Self-raising flour, plus extra for rolling out

2. 3 rounded teaspoons baking powder

3. 100g (4oz) soft margarine or butter, diced

4. 85g (3oz) caster sugar

5. 285 ml (half pint) buttermilk **or** runny natural yoghurt mixed with 1 tablespoon lemon juice

6. 1 free-range egg lightly beaten

Serve with home-made or high-fruit jam, and whipped double cream or clotted cream. Jam first, or cream first – depending on your preference.

This is the signature bake at Ardington. When our students hear the afternoon tea bell and gleefully drop their workshop materials to rush into the dining hall (not!) and see the cream teas lined up on the famous Ardington dresser, there are often little gasps of excitement. Ooooohs and Aaaahs exude – like bonfire night! Repeatedly, people say "These are so light! How on Earth do you get them like that?" This has been the main reason why we decided to put this book together. They are a secret family recipe, but we are happy to share it with you now because it's good to share. Ardington is all about sharing learning, and experiences, after all.

Top tips ~ there is no waste with this method as instead of cutting out circles and re-rolling any left-over dough, the scones are cut into equal squarish shapes using all the dough at the first pass. This ensures the dough doesn't get over worked and stodgy by re-rolling. The cooked scones also freeze really well, and respond beautifully to two to three minutes in a hot oven after defrosting, just before serving.

Method

Pre heat Fan oven 220°C. In a standard oven they may need 10 to 12 minutes at 220°C, gas mark 7, or Aga Roasting oven middle to upper runners.

Place items 1 to 4 in a large mixing bowl and, using a hand mixer, mix until well blended and looks like breadcrumbs (one minute or so). Mix items 5 and 6 together in a jug and whisk with a fork until combined. Add slowly to the main bowl and mix with your hand mixer for about 30 seconds or so until mostly combined. It will be a doughy clump but still just a little bit sticky.

Turn it onto a well-floured worktop, knead very lightly (no more than 20 seconds) and divide into two batches. Each batch makes 8 to 10 square scones (depending on how big you like them!). Quickly and gently shape each batch of the dough by hand into a rectangle about 3 cm thick. No need for a rolling pin or any degree of precision here….speed is of the essence. Cut the dough into roughly equal squarish scones. Place them on a baking sheet ready to go into the hot oven.

Bake: 8 to 10 minutes in fan oven. 10-12 minutes in a standard oven or Aga.

Ardington Cheese and Herb Scones

Makes 2 batches of 10 to 12 scones

1. 500g (1lb 2oz) self-raising flour (and extra for rolling)

2. 1 teaspoon salt

3. 3 rounded teaspoons baking powder

4. 2 rounded teaspoons dried basil

5. 1 rounded teaspoon dried thyme

6. 125g (5oz) butter or margarine, chopped into small chunks

7. 2 grinds of black pepper

8. 150g 6oz) grated strong cheddar cheese

9. 300ml (generous half pint) buttermilk **or** runny natural yoghurt including 1 tablespoon of lemon juice

10. 1 free-range egg

This is a savoury version of the classic Ardington Scone, using the same buttermilk approach to give that creamy taste and lightness.

Top tips ~ As with the classic scones, there is no waste with this method as instead of cutting out circles and re-rolling any left-over dough, the scones are cut into equal squarish shapes using all the dough at the first pass. This ensures the dough doesn't get over worked and stodgy by re-rolling. The cooked scones also freeze really well, and respond beautifully to two to three minutes in a hot oven after defrosting, just before serving. Great served with a bowl of home-made soup.

Method

Place items 1 to 8 in a large mixing bowl and, using a hand mixer, mix until well blended and looks like breadcrumbs (one minute or so). Mix items 9 and 10 together in a jug and whisk with a fork until combined. Add slowly to the main bowl and mix with your hand mixer for about 30 secs or so until mostly combined. It will be a doughy clump but still just a little bit sticky.

Turn it onto a well-floured worktop, knead very lightly (no more than 20 seconds) and divide into two batches. Each batch makes 8 to 10 square scones (depending on how big you like them!). Quickly and gently shape each batch of the dough by hand into a rectangle about 3 cm thick. No need for a rolling pin or any degree of precision here....speed is of the essence. Cut the dough into roughly equal squarish scones. Place them on a baking sheet ready to go into the hot oven.

Bake: 10 to 12 minutes in pre-heated oven 220 degrees C, Gas mark 7, Aga roasting oven on middle to upper runners.

Serve with a chunk of stilton or strong cheddar cheese and a side helping of chutney. Our favourite is a lovely Beetroot and Ginger Chutney, (this recipe can be found later in the book).

Ardington Soda Bread

Makes 1 loaf which cuts into about 24 pieces

1. 300g (10oz) self-raising white flour

2. 180g (6oz) wholemeal flour

3. ½ level teaspoon salt

4. 1 rounded teaspoon bicarbonate of soda

5. 300ml (generous half pint) buttermilk **or** runny natural yoghurt including 1 tablespoon of lemon juice

This is a loaf version of the savoury scone, using the same buttermilk approach to give that creamy taste and lightness.

Top tips – For a soft crust, wrap the loaf in a tea-towel and turn it upside down to cool once you bring it out of the oven. For a crisp crust, allow to cool right side up on a cooling rack. You can use a combination of white and wholemeal flours to suit your taste. Using all white flour makes a lighter loaf. Using all wholemeal flour makes it very heavy.

Method

Pre-heat oven 220°C, gas mark 7, Aga roasting oven on middle to upper runners.

Place all items into a large mixing bowl and bring together to combine well, with a large metal spoon or your hand. This shouldn't take longer than a minute or two.

Turn onto a well-floured worktop, knead very lightly (no more than 20 seconds) and bring it into a round flat shape about 5cm / 2 inches thick. Turn upside down (the base is usually neater and flatter) onto a floured baking tray and using a serrated bread knife, cut a deep cross in the top. Don't go right through the dough, but almost. It will split nicely during baking into four 'farls'.

Bake: 25 to 30 minutes.

Serve with a chunk of good flavoured cheese and a side helping of chutney. Our favourite is a lovely home-made Beetroot and Ginger Chutney, and the recipe can be found later in the book.

Ardington Stem Ginger Slices

Makes around 24 slices

For the cake~

1. 335g (12oz) butter or margarine, softened
2. 170g (6oz) light muscovado sugar (or dark muscovado for a stronger flavour)
3. 170g (6oz) granulated sugar
4. 420g (15 oz) self-raising flour
5. 2 rounded teaspoons baking powder
6. 2 – 4 rounded teaspoons ground ginger depending on how strong you like it
7. 5 free-range free-range eggs
8. 5 pieces stem ginger from a jar, finely chopped (don't overdo it or the cake goes soggy)

For the icing~

9. 280g (10oz) icing sugar, sieved
10. 5 tablespoons stem ginger syrup from the jar
11. 3 pieces stem ginger from a jar, chopped coarsely

Topping: Optional top with a sprinkle of sugar with piped whipped cream or a heaped teaspoon of clotted cream

This is a traybake recipe. When you are baking for up to 150 people per week, this is a particularly efficient way of making cakes. Like the cookie dough recipe, it is also very simple and versatile. It's the same basic recipe but lots of different extra ingredients can really change the look and taste of the cake.

Top tip ~ for a richer, stronger flavour and a darker cake, use a darker brown sugar. As stem ginger can be sometimes hard to find, you can also use 5 cubes of crystallised ginger, cut into small chunks and mixed through – don't get carried away and add more than this as it will cause the cake to sink and can overpower the flavour.

Method

Pre-heat fan oven 180°C, or standard oven to 200°C, gas mark 5, Aga baking oven on middle runners

Line a large rectangular tin with Bake-o-Glide, greaseproof paper, or simply grease it well with butter or margarine. The tins we use are either large Aga roasting tins 25cm x 35 cm, or a large brownie style baking tin 23cm x 33cm, which is about 9cm deep.

Measure all the cake ingredients 1 to 8 into a large mixing bowl and beat well with a hand mixer for about two minutes until well blended, and lighter in colour and texture. Turn the mixture into the prepared tin, using a silicon spatula to scrape every last bit out of the bowl. Bake in the preheated oven for about 25 to 30 minutes, until nicely browned and it springs back to the touch.

To make the icing, mix the icing sugar (9) and ginger syrup (10) together in a small bowl until smooth and a spreading consistency. Pour the icing over the cake while it is still warm (not hot), and spread gently to the edges with a small palette knife. Sprinkle with the chopped stem ginger (11) to decorate.

Allow the icing to set before slicing the tray bake to serve. This makes 24 slices and freezes very well.

Bake: 25-30 minutes.

Ardington Chocolate & Cacao Nibs Flapjacks

Makes 24 slices

1. 250g (9oz) real butter (or vegetable spread for a dairy-free version)
2. 180g (6oz) golden syrup (or swap some for honey)
3. 180g (6oz) light muscovado sugar
4. 500g (1lb 2oz) rolled oats (gluten free oats if required)
5. Extra ingredients: for these flapjacks use 50g (2oz) of Cacao nibs
6. Optional extras use other ingredients such as:

   100g (4oz)raisins, **or** 100g (4oz) desiccated coconut **or** 100g (4oz) chopped walnuts, or 100g (4oz) chopped glace cherries **or** 100g (4oz) dried apples / fruit **or** 100g (4oz) chocolate chips. Combine any of these in smaller proportions to make up 100g if you want a mix.
7. 200g (8oz) bar of chocolate, melted, to drizzle over the top after baking.

Flapjacks are a great gluten free option and can be made dairy-free too, so they are a good staple sweet option. Some don't really feel these are 'cakes' however, so when we serve them at Ardington, they are generally as an alternative along with 'real cake'. In the recipe below, we suggest all sort of extra ingredients you can add to the basic recipe to make them your own. These are Simon's second favourite cake.

Top tip – Bake them a few minutes longer for a really crispy and toffee-flavoured flapjack or a few minutes shorter if you prefer them a bit chewier.

Method

Pre-heated oven at 200°C, gas mark 6, Aga baking oven on top runners

Line a large rectangular tin with Bake-o-Glide, greaseproof paper, or simply grease it well with butter or margarine. The tins we use are either large Aga roasting tins 25cm x 35 cm, or a large brownie style baking tin 23cm x 33cm, which is about 9cm deep.

Combine the butter, syrup, and sugar, (1 to 3), in a large saucepan and heat gently until the ingredients have melted and combined. It should look quite liquid. Stir in the oats (4) off the heat, and add any other ingredients you have chosen (5) & (6) and mix well to combine thoroughly.

Spoon into the prepared tin and press down with the back of a metal spoon. Bake in a pre-heated oven until browned and slightly sizzling. Drizzle with melted chocolate (7) and slice into pieces once baked and partly cooled.

Bake: 20 to 25 minutes in pre-heated oven at 200C, Gas mark 6, Aga baking oven on top runners

Ardington Lemon and Lime Drizzle Cake

Makes around 24 slices

For the cake~

1. 5 free-range eggs

2. 335g (12oz) soft margarine or butter

3. 335g (12oz) caster sugar

4. 420g (15oz) self-raising flour

5. 6 tablespoons milk

6. 2 level teaspoons baking powder

7. Grated rind and juice of 2 lemons and 2 limes

8. 1 teaspoon lemon oil

Glaze (pour on hot cake after removing from tin)~

9. 6 tablespoons lemon and / or lime juice and 1 teaspoon lemon oil

10. 225g (8oz) granulated sugar

This one is what Simon calls a 'Premier League Cake'. It's always a hit and gets chosen over other options.

Top tip – an easier option than grating fresh lemons and limes is to have a bottle of good lemon and / or lime juice in the fridge, and a lemon oil essence in the cupboard. In can take ten minutes off the preparation time if you need a Lemon Drizzle cake in a rush!

Method

Pre-heat fan oven to 180°C, or in a standard oven 200°C, gas mark 6, Aga baking oven on middle runners.

Line a large rectangular tin with Bake-o-Glide, greaseproof paper, or simply grease it well with butter or margarine. The tins we use are either the large Aga roasting tins, 25cm x 35 cm, or a large brownie style baking tin, 23cm x 33cm, which is about 9cm deep.

Measure all the cake ingredients (1 to 8) into a large bowl and beat well with a mixer for about two minutes until well blended, and lighter in colour and texture. Turn the mixture into the prepared tin, using a silicon spatula to scrape every last bit out of the bowl. Bake in the preheated oven for about 25 to 30 minutes, until nicely browned and it springs back to the touch.

To make the glaze, mix the juice (9) and sugar (10) together in a small bowl until smooth. Pour the glaze over the cake while still quite hot, spreading gently to the edges with a small palette knife.

Allow the glaze to set before slicing the tray bake to serve. This makes 24 slices and freezes very well.

Bake: 25-30 minutes.

Ardington Coffee & Walnut (or Pecan) Squares

For the cake~

1. 5 free-range eggs
2. 335g (12oz) soft margarine or softened butter
3. 335g (12oz) caster sugar
4. 420g (15oz) self-raising flour
5. 2 level teaspoons baking powder
6. 170g (6oz) chopped walnut or pecan pieces
7. 5 teaspoons instant coffee mixed with 1 tablespoon hot water into a paste

For the icing~

8. 170g (6oz) soft margarine or softened butter
9. 3 teaspoons instant coffee and hot water as above (allow to cool slightly)
10. 335g (12oz) icing sugar sieved
11. walnut or pecan pieces to decorate (see also Top Tip)

Another premier league special. Even coffee haters like the subtler taste of a nice slice of coffee cake.

Top tip – if the walnuts or pecans are crushed and sprinkled on the top, instead of arranged 'one half walnut per piece of cake', then it makes the large full cake easier to divide into various sized pieces. The icing can split if you put the hot coffee mix onto room temperature butter, so always use cold (as in straight from the fridge) butter / spread and cool the coffee mix

Method

Pre-heat fan oven 180°C, standard oven 200°C / gas mark 6, Aga baking oven on middle runners.

Line a large rectangular tin with Bake-o-Glide, greaseproof paper, or simply grease it well with butter or margarine. The tins we use are either the large Aga roasting tins, 25cm x 35 cm, or a large brownie style baking tin, 23cm x 33cm, which is about 9cm deep.

Measure all the cake ingredients (1 to 7) into a large bowl and beat well with a mixer for about two minutes until well blended, and lighter in colour and texture. Turn the mixture into the prepared tin, using a silicon spatula to scrape every last bit out of the bowl. Bake in the preheated oven for about 25 to 30 minutes, until nicely browned and it springs back to the touch.

To make the icing, mix the butter, coffee and icing sugar (8 to 10) together in a bowl with a hand mixer until smooth. When the cake is completely cool, put the icing onto the top spreading gently to the edges with a small palette knife. Decorate with walnut halves (11). Cut into 24 squares.

Bake: 25-30 minutes.

Ardington Sultana and Orange Slices

Makes around 24 slices

1. 5 free-range eggs

2. 335g (12oz) softened butter or soft margarine

3. 335g (12oz) caster sugar

4. 420g (15oz) self-raising flour

5. 2 level teaspoons baking powder

6. 3 tablespoons fresh orange juice

7. Grated rind of 3 oranges

8. 2 teaspoons of orange oil

9. 225g (8oz) sultanas

10. Demerara sugar to sprinkle on after baking for topping

This cake also makes a great warm sponge cake to serve with custard, and is one of the simplest of bakes to make. The crispy crust of Demerara sugar works really well with the zesty orange flavour.

Method

Pre-heat fan oven 180 degrees, standard oven 200°C / gas mark 6, Aga baking oven on middle runners.

Line a large rectangular tin with Bake-o-Glide, greaseproof paper, or simply grease it well with butter or margarine. The tins we use are either the large Aga roasting tins, 25cm x 35 cm, or a large brownie style baking tin, 23cm x 33cm, which is about 9cm deep.

Measure all the cake ingredients (1 to 9) into a large bowl and beat well with a mixer for about two minutes until well blended, and lighter in colour and texture. Turn the mixture into the prepared tin, using a silicon spatula to scrape every last bit out of the bowl. Bake in the preheated oven for about 25 to 30 minutes, until nicely browned and it springs back to the touch.

Sprinkle a good layer of Demerara sugar onto cake whilst still warm, then cut into slices.

Bake: 25-30 minutes.

Ardington Triple Chocolate Biscuit, Walnut & Raisin Tiffin

Serves 24 - best straight from the fridge

For the cake ~

1. 8 tablespoons golden syrup

2. 335g (12oz) real butter

3. 280g (10oz) broken chocolate – use a mixture of white, dark and milk

4. 450g (16oz) crushed digestive biscuits (put in plastic bag and bash with a rolling pin to crush)

5. 225g (8oz) crushed rich tea biscuits (put in plastic bag and bash with a rolling pin to crush)

6. 225g (8oz) roughly chopped walnuts

7. 335g (12oz) raisins

For the topping ~

8. 200g (8oz) melted chocolate to drizzle onto the top – use a mixture of white, dark and milk chocolate

Tiffin is another interesting one – like flapjacks. There are those that don't believe this is a 'real cake'. At Ardington, Tiffin is sometimes cut into small bite-sized chunks and used as an after lunch fudge or toffee alternative. That's if it makes it to the dining room dresser of course – it's Simon's favourite and often doesn't see the light of an Ardington day. He will eat it straight out of the freezer.

Top tips ~ the chocolate and biscuit pieces in here need to be big enough to taste and add texture, so don't chop them any smaller than a raisin. You can use premium chocolates to make this recipe really special.

Method

No cooking required.

Line a large rectangular tin with Bake-o-Glide, greaseproof paper, or simply grease it well with butter or margarine. The tins we use are either the large Aga roasting tins, 25cm x 35 cm, or a large brownie style baking tin, 23cm x 33cm, which is about 9cm deep.

Melt the chocolate, butter and syrup (1 to 3) together in a large heatproof bowl over a pan of hot water, or in a large saucepan in the warming oven of the Aga. Add all the other Tiffin ingredients (4 to 7) and mix well with a wooden spoon to combine. Press firmly into the prepared tin using the back of a metal spoon. Drizzle on the melted chocolate (8) to coat, using the three different coloured chocolates to make a lovely marbled effect on top. No cooking required.

Chill in the fridge until set and then cut into squares or slices, or mini pieces to fill your sweet jar.

Ardington Chocolate Brownies

Makes 24 pieces

① 400g (14oz) caster sugar

② 300g (11oz) melted butter (or you can use a vegetable spread for a dairy free version)

③ 400g (14oz) dark muscovado sugar

④ 90g (3oz) cocoa powder

⑤ 1 teaspoon vanilla extract

⑥ 5 free-range eggs

⑦ 150g (6oz) plain flour (or gluten free flour)

⑧ 1 level teaspoon baking powder (gluten free version if needed)

⑨ 1/2 teaspoon salt

⑩ 60g (2oz) walnut halves or chocolate chips

These are a great gluten free option as the flour content is so low, it is easy to replace with a GF flour, and you do not lose any of the structure of the finished brownie, as you can with some GF recipes.

Top tip – these are lovely served warm as a dessert, topped with ice cream. There are plenty of recipes that make brownies quite hard work – ours is a tried and tested all in one special again.

Method:

Pre-heat oven 180°C, gas mark 5, Aga baking oven middle to lower runners.

Line a large rectangular tin with Bake-o-Glide, greaseproof paper, or simply grease it well with butter or margarine. The tins we use are either the large Aga roasting tins, 25cm x 35 cm, or a large brownie style baking tin, 23cm x 33cm, which is about 9cm deep.

Place all ingredients (1 to 10) into a large mixing bowl and mix with a hand mixer until well combined. Pour into the prepared tin. Bake in the preheated oven for about 25 minutes. It's not always easy to tell if your brownies are cooked as they can look and feel squidgy. If the centre wobbles when you look after 25 minutes, then keep them in the oven for another five minutes or so. They should develop a papery crust and will also have started to shrink slightly around the edges.

Cool, and slice into 24 equal square portions.

Bake: 25 minutes then check them. They may need another 5-10 minutes if not set.

Ardington Carrot Cake with Cinnamon Frosting

Makes 24 slices or squares

For the cake~

1. 375ml (14 fluid oz) sunflower oil
2. 6 large free-range eggs
3. 350g (12oz) dark muscovado sugar
4. 2 teaspoons of orange essence
5. 300g (10oz) carrots, coarsely grated
6. 125g (5oz) walnuts
7. 450g (1lb) self-raising flour
8. 3 teaspoons baking powder
9. 2 teaspoons cinnamon
10. 1 teaspoon ground ginger

For the cinnamon frosting~

11. 170g (6oz) butter, room temperature / softish
12. 335g (12oz) icing sugar
13. 2 teaspoons cinnamon
14. Grated zest of an orange to decorate on top of frosting

A premier league cake, and with a frosting that freezes well.

Top tip ~ it is more traditional to use a cream cheese based frosting to top a carrot cake. That's nice but it doesn't freeze well, so eat it fresh if you go that route!

Method

Pre-heat fan oven 180°C, standard oven 200°C / gas mark 6, Aga baking oven on middle to upper runners.

Line a large rectangular tin with Bake-o-Glide, greaseproof paper, or simply grease it well with butter or margarine. The tins we use are either the large Aga roasting tins, 25cm x 35 cm, or a large brownie style baking tin, 23cm x 33cm, which is about 9cm deep.

Put the oil, free-range eggs, sugar and orange essence (1 to 4) into a large mixing bowl. Whisk with a hand mixer until the mixture is well combined, lighter, and somewhat thickened. Gently fold the carrot and walnuts (5 and 6) into the cake batter, then gently sieve in (all at once) the flour, baking powder, cinnamon and ginger (7 to 10) folding until evenly blended. Pour into the prepared tin and bake for 40 to 45 minutes in a pre-heated oven, until it springs back when touched.

Make a cinnamon butter frosting by mixing (11 to 13) in a large mixing bowl with a hand mixer. Whisk until light and frothy – about 2 mins max. Apply the frosting to the top of the cake with a palette knife, smoothing gently to the edges. Cut into 24 slices or squares. Decorate with grated orange zest just before serving.

Bake: 40 to 45 minutes.

Ardington Rich Chocolate Cake

Serves around 16 pieces, depending on how generous you are.

1. 225g (8oz) self-raising flour or gluten free flour

2. 150g (6oz) caster sugar

3. 40g (1.5 oz) cocoa

4. 1.5 rounded teaspoons bicarbonate of soda

5. 200ml (7fl oz) milk

6. 3 large free-range eggs

7. 100ml (3.5fl oz) vegetable oil

8. 4 drops vanilla essence

9. 2 tablespoons of black treacle

10. Half a jar of good jam to sandwich the two cakes together

This is the recipe Yvonne was taught at school, and has been a family favourite for decades. All generations in the Sonsino line rely on this slightly sticky, moist cake for special occasions – from Great Grandmother (and father) down to Great granddaughters (and son). It has to be the easiest chocolate cake recipe ever, and as you will see, is dairy free and can be made gluten free with success. We hope you enjoy it.

Top Tips ~ Sandwich the two cakes together with stoned and halved black cherries that have been simmered until tender with a little sugar, then cover this cake in a thick layer of whipped double cream to make a vintage classic Black Forest gateau. Heap another pile of the black cherry coulis on top and grate dark chocolate over just before serving.

If you heat your tablespoon gently over a gas flame, the black treacle comes off cleanly when you dip it into the tin. Do take care to use appropriate oven gloves to avoid burning yourself.

Method:

Pre-heat fan oven to 180°C or standard oven at 170°C / gas mark 4, Aga baking oven on grid shelf on floor.

Line the bases and grease two 8 to 9 inch sandwich tins.

Sieve all the dry ingredients (1 to 4) together into a bowl and make a well in the centre. Mix all the wet ingredients (5 to 9), in a jug and whisk with a fork to combine well. Pour into the dry ingredients well, and stir with a metal spoon (like stirring a cup of tea). When all ingredients are thoroughly combined (30 seconds or so of stirring), pour the runny cake mixture in equal measures into the two prepared sandwich tins and bake for 30 minutes in the pre-heated oven. The cakes will be well risen and springy to the touch when ready.

Leave to cool on a cooling rack and sandwich together with the jam.(10)

Bake: 30-35 minutes in a fan oven or 35-40 minutes in a standard oven.

Ardington Cherry & Coconut Shortbread Cake

For the shortbread~

1. 120g (5oz) sour cherries, chopped small
2. 250g (9oz) salted butter, at room temperature
3. 120g (5oz) cornflour
4. 240g (9oz) plain flour (or substitute gluten free flour)
5. 120g (5oz) golden caster sugar
6. 100g (4oz) desiccated coconut

For the coconut cake topping~

7. 3 free-range eggs
8. 170g (6oz) butter or margarine
9. 170g (6oz) caster sugar
10. 200g (7oz) self-raising flour
11. 1 tablespoon milk
12. 2 level teaspoons baking powder
13. 100g (4oz) desiccated coconut

This one is a little more time consuming to bake as it consists of a shortbread underlayer and a sponge cake top. Good though!

Top tips – You can make each layer as a separate cake if you don't want to combine it. The shortbread makes a great gluten free biscuit option if you substitute all of the flours as shown. You could also vary the flavourings – replace the coconut and cherries with other fruit or chocolate chips etc.

Method

Pre-heat oven at 180°C, gas mark 5, Aga baking oven on middle to lower runners.

Line a large rectangular tin with Bake-o-Glide, greaseproof paper, or simply grease it well with butter or margarine. The tins we use are either the large Aga roasting tins, 25cm x 35 cm, or a large brownie style baking tin, 23cm x 33cm, which is about 9cm deep.

Shortbread underlayer: Add all the shortbread ingredients (1 to 6) to a large mixing bowl, and mix with a hand mixer until the mixture just comes together. Press into the base of the prepared baking tin and bake in a pre-heated oven for 10 minutes. Allow to cool.

Cake topping: Put all the cake ingredients (7 to 13) into mixing bowl and mix with the hand mixer until well combined and looking lighter in colour and texture (no more than a couple of minutes). Spread evenly, with a palette knife, on top of the shortbread base.

Bake in a pre-heated oven for about 30 to 35 minutes until golden brown and the top springs back lightly when touched. Sprinkle with more coconut and granulated sugar while still hot.

Bake: 30 to 35 minutes. When cooled cut into 24 squares or slices

Ardington Chocolate and Almond Marbled Bundt Cake

Serves around 12-16

1. 185g (7oz) butter, softened, plus extra for greasing

2. 240g (9oz) caster sugar

3. 1 teaspoon almond extract

4. 1 teaspoon baking powder

5. 200g (8oz) self-raising flour

6. 75g (3oz) ground almonds

7. 3 large free-range eggs

8. 2 tablespoons milk

9. 3 tablespoons cocoa powder mixed with 3 tablespoon hot water to make a paste

10. 30g icing sugar, to dust cake when ready to serve

The Bundt style cake tin is usually a decorative, round tin with a hole in the centre, which helps it bake more quickly and evenly. You can use ordinary cake tins if you prefer.

Method

Pre-heat oven to 180°C, gas mark 5, Aga baking oven on middle to lower runners.

Grease a 1.5 litre Bundt (decorative) tin carefully. Measure the main cake ingredients (1 to 8) in a large mixing bowl and using all in one whisk approach, whisk with a hand mixer for a minute or two until the mixture looks lighter in colour and texture. In a separate medium sized bowl, mix the cocoa powder with hot water (9) until combined into a paste. Then divide the cake mixture into two, putting one half into the chocolate paste bowl, and fold well until thoroughly combined. Spoon your two mixtures into the Bundt tin in alternative dollops, swirling a little so that you create a marbled effect. Bake in pre-heated oven until well risen and springs back to the touch.

Bake~for around 30 to 35 minutes

Almond and Blackcurrant Tart– The 'Ardington Bakewell'

Serves abound 12

For the pie crust and base ~

1. 200g (7oz) plain flour

2. 90g (3oz) cold butter or margarine, cut into smallish chunks

3. 2 tablespoons cold water

4. 2 heaped tablespoons blackcurrant jam

Almost everyone loves a Bakewell Tart, and this is our take on it. Made with Blackcurrant jam (home-made if you can as the fruit texture and flavour are just so much more intense), it always goes very quickly when served at the school.

Top tips ~ for speed, frozen pastry is a good alternative. Making two or more at a time can be useful – they freeze really well! If you prefer a less sweet version, only make up one third of the icing amount, including the blackcurrant jam, and drizzle it over the finished and cooled tart.

Method

Pre heat oven to 180ºC, gas mark 5, Aga baking oven, middle shelf.

First make the short-crust pastry base. Sieve the flour into a mixing bowl, add the butter and rub lightly with just the tips of the fingers until it resembles breadcrumbs (1 and 2). Don't overwork it or let it get too warm, so work quickly with cold hands and utensils. Add the cold water (3) and bring the mixture together into a ball either with your hands or a metal spatula or spoon. It should be soft but not sticky. Rest it in the fridge for half an hour.

Use this chilled pastry to line a 9 inch (23cm) flan tin or quiche dish, by rolling it out on a floured worktop until just a little bigger than the diameter and depth of the baking tin. For example, if you are using a 9 inch wide tin that is one inch deep, roll your pastry into a 12 inch circle. Lift carefully over your rolling pin and lay into the dish, carefully pressing up the sides of the dish to cover it well. Trim off any excess pastry, add a circle of greaseproof paper or a layer of clingfilm over the pastry base and then weigh that down with baking beans. Bake blind for 10 – 15 minutes. Remove the baking beans and paper or cling film and then return to the oven to bake for another 10 minutes. Remove from the oven and allow to cool slightly, then spread the blackcurrant jam in the base of the tart case.

For the almond sponge filling and icing ~ over the page ☞

Almond and Blackcurrant Tart – The 'Ardington Bakewell'
continued

For the almond sponge filling~

⑤ 125g (5oz) butter, melted (then the batter pours easily)

⑥ 125g (5oz) light brown muscovado or caster sugar

⑦ 100g (4oz) ground almonds

⑧ 25g (1oz) custard powder

⑨ 2 large free-range eggs, beaten

⑩ half teaspoon almond extract

For the icing~

⑪ 250g (9oz) icing sugar

⑫ half teaspoon almond extract

⑬ 2 to 3 tablespoons cold water

⑭ 1 teaspoon sieved blackcurrant jam

To make the almond sponge filling, measure all the filling ingredients (5 to 10) into a mixing bowl and using a hand mixer, beat well for a minute or two until thoroughly combined and smooth. Pour into the tart case on top of the jam.

Bake for 25 – 35 minutes, until golden, slightly risen and no wobble.

Then, make a stiff icing. Place ingredients (11 to 13) into a bowl and mix with a hand mix until silky smooth. Place 1 tablespoon of this icing into a separate bowl and colour it with the sieved jam(14), mixing well. Spoon the white icing over the cooled tart. A bit running down the sides of the tart is encouraged! Put the blackcurrant icing into a small piping bag fitted with a no. 2 plain nozzle, and then drizzle parallel lines of it over your tart about 1 to 2 inches apart. Quickly and before it sets, create a marbled or feathered pattern with a cocktail stick, dragging it at right angles across your icing in alternative directions.

Leave to set.

Ardington Banana and Chocolate Loaf

Serves around 10 to 12 slices.

1. 100g (4oz) butter or margarine

2. 150g (6oz) dark muscovado sugar

3. 3 medium free-range eggs

4. 2 large ripe bananas fresh or frozen

5. 200g (8oz) self-raising flour

6. 1 teaspoon baking powder

7. 1 teaspoon cinnamon

8. 200g (8oz) bar cooking chocolate chopped into chunks

9. Whipped cream or butter for serving (optional)

Top tips ~ You can use frozen bananas for this. Any bananas sitting in the fruit bowl that are just a bit too ripe for eating freeze really well, and with a short time at room temperature, will thaw enough to be peeled and added to this cake. They will have turned black on the outside but this is normal. This is also delicious with the swiss style triangular chocolate with nuts in, cut up into bitesize chunks.

Method

Pre-heat oven 180°C, gas mark 5, Aga baking oven middle to lower runners.

Grease and line a 1 kg loaf tin or a long thin rectangular cake tin.

Cream the butter and sugar (1&2) in a mixing bowl using a hand whisk. Mix in the free-range eggs and the bananas (3&4). It will look a bit sloppy at this stage but don't worry. Fold in the flour, cinnamon and baking powder (5,6,7). Add the chopped chocolate (8) and mix well to combine. Pour into the prepared baking tin. Bake in a pre-heated oven for about 1 hour to 1 hour 10 minutes, until well risen and springs back when touched. This cake is great served slightly warm with whipped cream. Alternatively, it is good served sliced and cool, either plain or spread with butter.

Bake~1 hour to 1 hour 10 minutes. Serves around 8 to 10 slices. The long rectangular tins slice into around 12 slices.

Ardington Mince Pies

Makes 12 pies

① 375g (14oz) plain flour

② 125g (5oz) icing sugar

③ 260g (9oz) chilled unsalted butter, chopped

④ 1 egg

⑤ 410g (1lb) jar of really good mincemeat

⑥ Caster sugar to sprinkle on when baked

We can sell more than 200 of these in an afternoon, and have done so at each of our Winter Fairs so far. These have been described as 'the best mince pies I have ever tasted' on many occasions.

Top tips ~ Use a non-stick deep muffin tin for a lovely well-filled mince pie. This recipe uses a delicious sweet pastry, not rolled-out but pressed into the tins like a shortbread mix, which gives them a really textured and home-made feel.

Method:

Pre-heat oven to 200°C, gas Mark 6, or Aga baking oven middle to upper shelf

Make the sweet pastry by sieving the flour and sugar (1 and 2) into a bowl and rubbing in the butter (3) with just the fingertips until it resembles breadcrumbs. Add the egg (4) and mix to a dough. If the mixture feels too dry, add a tablespoon of cold water. Put into the fridge and chill for at least half an hour.

Set aside about one quarter of the pastry in the fridge to roll out for lids. Pull a small handful of pastry off from the remaining dough ball and press into one of the 12 moulds in a non-stick deep muffin tin. Cover the base and sides of each muffin tin to around 4mm, working quickly with the remaining pastry.

Add a good tablespoon of mincemeat to fill up each pie. Roll the remaining pastry and using a cutter, make 12 pie lids and put one on each pie. Fork them around the edges to seal and make a small hole in the top of each with a sharp knife.

Bake in a preheated oven until golden brown. Sprinkle with caster sugar to serve.

Bake~25 to 30 minutes. Serves 12

Ardington Marmalade Fruit Cake

Serves around 12 to 16 slices

1. 175g (6oz) butter or soft margarine, chopped

2. 175g (6oz) dark muscovado sugar

3. 350g (12oz) mixed dried fruit of your choice – sultanas, raisins, chopped peel, chopped apricots, chopped prunes, glace cherries, papaya etc

4. 3 large free-range eggs

5. 250g (10oz) self-raising flour (or gluten free flour)

6. 1 heaped tablespoon of marmalade

7. 1 piece of fresh fruit to slice and arrange on top of cake before baking

8. Drizzle of golden syrup or honey to glaze fruit after baking (no more than a level tablespoon)

This is not a heavy fruit cake – it's more of an afternoon tea style fruit cake. It does well as a gluten free version too.

Top tip: Don't overdo the marmalade, even though it's tempting to, as it makes the cake a bit wet and the fruit can sink. Arranging fruit on the top of this cake makes it a bit special, and there's usually a spare apple or peach or orange in the fruit bowl that will do nicely.

Method:

Pre-heat oven to 170°C, gas mark 4, Aga baking oven with the grid shelf on the floor.

Grease and line a round 20cm (8 inch) cake tin.

Measure all cake ingredients (1 to 6) into a large mixing bowl and whisk for a minute or two with a hand blender until all ingredients are thoroughly combined. Tip into the prepared cake tin and smooth flat with a spatula. Slice your piece of fruit (7) and arrange on the top of the cake.

Bake in a pre-heated oven until nicely browned and it springs back to the touch. Leave to partially cool in the tin and drizzle with syrup or honey (8). Keeps well in a storage tin and cuts better when it is a day or so old.

Bake: 1 hour 30 minutes

Ardington White Chocolate & Raspberry Cheesecake

Serves up to 16 slices

1 1 pack (approx. 250g / 9oz) digestive biscuits, crushed

2 150g unsalted butter, melted

For the filling ~

3 500g (1lb) white chocolate, broken into pieces

4 75g (3oz) unsalted butter

5 1 teaspoon vanilla essence

6 500g (1lb) cream cheese

7 50g (2oz) icing sugar

8 180ml (6 fluid ounces) whipping cream

9 1 punnet fresh raspberries or equivalent of frozen / tinned

Top tips ~ For a less rich (less calorific) version of this you can replace all or some of the cream cheese for a light quark version of soft cheese. You do lose some of the flavour too however. You can also change the digestive biscuit base for ginger nuts or hobnobs or gluten free biscuits to suit diet and preferences, as well as change raspberries for another soft fruit. Our preference is the raspberries with white chocolate as they are a particularly good combination. Make sure the base is completely solid before you add the filling, as it doesn't make a good finish to have biscuit crumbs in a beautifully smooth cheesecake. The bowl for melting the chocolate gets very hot so be sure to keep an eye on it. The residual heat in the bowl will continue to melt the chocolate once its removed from the heat and can burn which will make it grainy.

Method:

Make the base first by mixing together items 1 and 2. We tend to crush the biscuits by putting them in a robust plastic bag and bashing them with a wooden rolling pin. Press into the bottom of a shallow flan tin (20 to 25cm diameter) to make a thin even layer. Chill well in fridge.

Measure the white chocolate, butter and vanilla (3 to 5) into a heatproof bowl and set over a pan of gently simmering water, ensuring the bowl doesn't touch the water. Once the chocolate and butter have melted, remove the bowl from the heat (see top tips), and stir until smooth. In a separate bowl, mix together the cream cheese, icing sugar and whipping cream (6 to 8) till smooth. Add your melted chocolate mixture to this, stirring very well and quickly, as the chocolate will begin to set as it hits the cold cheese. A hand mixer would do this nicely. Gently fold in about three quarters of your raspberries (9). Tinned or frozen will leave a raspberry trail in your cake – it can look quite nice.

Finally, pour this filling mix over your biscuit base and chill in the fridge overnight. Decorate with the remaining raspberries just before serving.

Preserves

Beetroot Ginger
Chutney
30/7/22

Ardington Beetroot and Ginger Chutney

Makes 5 to 6 1lb jars

1. 675g (1.5lbs) of chopped red onion

2. 1.1 litres (2 pints) white vinegar which keeps the beetroot colour better

3. 1.5kg (3lbs) of cooked, peeled beetroot, cut into small chunks

4. 675g (1.5lbs) apples, peeled, cored and chopped

5. 3 heaped tablespoons ground ginger

6. 1 heaped teaspoon salt

7. 900g (2lbs) granulated sugar

We have been making this for many years with home grown produce. Beetroot has been a favourite to grow since early childhood – watching the fat purple roots develop during the growing season, combined with the earthy smell of it cooking on the stove, bring back fond memories. This chutney combines fruit and vegetables that all mature at the same time in Autumn, so is a great way of using up the odd shaped produce that doesn't make it to the salad or fruit bowl.

Top tips ~ As with any chutney, the flavour develops as it matures. Try and hide a few jars in the back of the cupboard for two or three years as the flavour will be spectacular. Careful jar preparation will ensure it remains in perfect condition. We always warm the jars in the oven on a paper lined tray as part of the sterilisation process, and then they are ready for pouring in the chutney while it is still hot. The steam will push air out through the screwed on lid, creating a good vacuum seal. If you have done this right, you will hear the jar lid 'pop' as the chutney cools.

Method

Put the onion and half the vinegar (1 and 2) into a large preserving pan and simmer gently until the onion starts to soften. Add the beetroot, apples, ginger and salt, and half the remaining vinegar and simmer until pulpy – this may take up to 20 minutes or so. If you like a smoother chutney, use a potato masher during this simmering process to squash your chutney into the desired consistency. We leave it mostly chunky.

Finally, add the sugar and remaining vinegar, stirring well, and continue cooking until thick again. Allow to cool slightly – five to ten minutes should do. Pot into sterilised jars and seal with a vinegar proof lid.

Leave at least six to eight weeks to mature.

Ardington Rhubarb and Rose Petal Jam

Makes around 5 x 1lb jars

1. 1.3kg (3lbs) of rhubarb, cut into 2cm (1 inch) slices

2. 1.3kg (3lbs) of jam sugar (with pectin, as rhubarb does not naturally have good enough quantities of this)

3. 225g (8oz) rose petals

This is a joy to make because the delicate fragrances of the rhubarb and rose petals are a sensory delight. The colours are an artistic inspiration too.

Top tips ~ Find the strongest scented roses that you can and gather the petals before they drop. A mixture of pink, white and red colours is fine but don't be tempted to add yellow as the jam will go a bit brown looking. The rhubarb should be hearty allotment style, picked in June before it goes too stringy, but still has plenty of flavour. Making jam is as much an art as a science – setting point is the most difficult thing to get right and it requires trial and error. You need to get a balance with good colour and just set enough to spoon and spread. A preferred method is suggested below.

Method

Put all ingredients (1 to 3) into a large preserving pan and heat gently, stirring almost continuously with a long handled wooden spoon until all the sugar has dissolved. You can 'hear' if there are still sugar crystals in the mixture as you use the wooden spoon to stir. Be patient and let it all melt out.

Bring up to a rapid boil (this is when you know you really needed the large preserving pan as it will more than double in size) until setting point is reached. The jam sugar may have guidelines on the packet in which case use those as a guide. It could take anywhere between 5 and 25 minutes or more. Stir occasionally during rapid boil and make sure you wear a long oven glove to protect your hand and arm from hot jam splashes.

My tried and tested method for finding the perfect setting point is to do the cold plate test: put a small plate in the freezer before you start to make the jam. Test for setting point by placing a small drizzle of jam on the cold plate. Push it with your finger nail and if it 'wrinkles' then it is at setting point. Test it first after five minutes, then again after another five etc, until you can feel that wrinkle is wrinkly enough! Keep the plate in the freezer between tests. Don't overboil the jam as it goes tough and crystalises.

Once setting point is reached, cool for five minutes and then pot up into sterilised jars. Careful jar preparation will ensure it remains in perfect condition. We always warm the jars in the oven on a paper lined tray as part of the sterilisation process, and then they are ready for pouring in the jam while it is still hot. The steam will push air out through the screwed on lid, creating a good vacuum seal. If you have done this right, you will hear the jar lid 'pop' as the jam cools.

Ardington Strawberry Jam

Makes around 8 x 1lb jars

① 2kg (4.5lbs) slightly underripe strawberries, with very large ones cut in half and small ones kept whole

② 2kg (4.5lbs) jam sugar with pectin

Home grown strawberries work best in this recipe. They are often the oddest shapes therefore not ideal for the table, plus you can collect them at the peak stage for jam making – just before they are too ripe. If there is a little bit of green on them, they are slightly more acid and help with setting. Alternatively it's a great adventure to visit a pick your own farm to gather them in quantity especially for the jam pot.

Top tips ~ Always use equal quantities of fruit and jam sugar. Normal recipes have more sugar than fruit, but I never make it like that. I also like the fruit to stay in big chunks so not much chopping or mashing goes on in the process for me. For a smoother jam, chop or mash the fruit accordingly.

Method

Put fruit and sugar (1&2) into a large preserving pan and heat gently, stirring almost continuously with a long handled wooden spoon until all the sugar has dissolved. You can 'hear' if there are still sugar crystals in the mixture as you use the wooden spoon to stir. Be patient and let it all melt out.

Bring up to a rapid boil (this is when you know you really needed the large preserving pan as it will more than double in size) until setting point is reached. The jam sugar may have guidelines on the packet in which case use those as a guide. It could take anywhere between 5 and 15 minutes or more. Stir occasionally during rapid boil and make sure you wear a long oven glove to protect your hand and arm from hot jam splashes.

My tried and tested method for finding the perfect setting point is to do the cold plate test: put a small plate in the freezer before you start to make the jam. Test for setting point by placing a small drizzle of jam on the cold plate. Push it with your finger nail and if it 'wrinkles' then it is at setting point. Test it first after five minutes, then again after another few minutes etc, until you can feel that wrinkle is wrinkly enough! Keep the plate in the freezer between tests. Don't overboil the jam as it goes tough and crystalises, and you will destroy the lovely colour and shape of the strawberries.

Once setting point is reached, cool for five minutes and then pot up into sterilised jars. Careful jar preparation will ensure it remains in perfect condition. We always warm the jars in the oven on a paper lined tray as part of the sterilisation process, and then they are ready for pouring in the jam while it is still hot. The steam will push air out through the screwed on lid, creating a good vacuum seal. If you have done this right, you will hear the jar lid 'pop' as the jam cools.

Ardington Piccalilli

Makes about 6 x 1lb jars

1. A large cauliflower, broken into small florets

2. 450g (1lb) shallots or pickling onions, cut in halves

3. 1.4 litres (2.5 pints) white vinegar

4. 900 g (2lbs) of other chopped mixed vegetables (green beans, cucumbers, courgettes, green tomatoes, yellow or green peppers, baby sweet corn, chillies if you like it hot)

5. 2 large garlic cloves, finely chopped

6. 450g (1lb) sugar

7. 50g (2oz) mustard powder

8. 25g (1oz) turmeric powder

9. 3 heaped teaspoons salt

10. 2 heaped teaspoons lightly ground coriander seeds

11. 115g (4oz) plain flour (or a gluten free alternative)

This is a good recipe if you are a vegetable gardener as you can put lots of your home grown misshapes in this recipe. The vegetables can be varied too, so you don't have to stick to the recipe.

Top tip ~ If you have a mustard allergy you can leave out the mustard powder in this recipe and still get a good flavoured pickle. Try and chop all your vegetables into the same size – smaller if you want to use as a sandwich spread or slightly larger if you like to serve it as a side chutney. You can also make this gluten free.

Method
In a large preserving pan, simmer the cauliflower and onions (1 and 2) in half the vinegar for ten minutes. Add items 4, 5 and 6 and continue to simmer for another ten minutes. In a separate bowl, mix all the dry ingredients (7 to 11) into a paste with a little of the remaining vinegar. Add the remaining vinegar to the main pan. Gently add the spice paste to the pan, stirring all the time to prevent lumps forming. Simmer for another five to ten minutes until nicely thickened. Pot into sterilised prepared jars with a vinegar proof seal.

Leave for a few weeks to mature before eating.

Orange Marmalade
9\2\19

marmal
Fed

Ardington Orange Marmalade

Makes about 6 or 7 1lb jars.

1 1.5kg (3lbs) Seville oranges

2 Juice of 2 lemons

3 2.6kg (5lbs) preserving sugar

This is a lovely recipe to make with family (especially grandchildren as in our case as you can see from the labels) as you can get them all to help! The lovely aromas of marmalade-in-motion fill the house.

Top tips ~ Seville oranges are the traditional bitter orange fruit used in marmalade making but you can make a lovely preserve from big Winter oranges, or a combination of citrus fruits including grapefruits, lemons, limes (don't get thin skinned ones). Adding a little drop of whiskey or a stick of cinnamon, or a few slices of ginger into a jar or two as you pot it up can provide a good selection of alternative flavoured preserves.

Method

This is made in two half batches but first you need to cook and soften all the oranges / fruit.

Put the whole oranges and lemon juice (1&2) in a large preserving pan and cover with water (around 3 pints or so). Weight down the oranges with a heat-proof plate to keep them submerged. Bring to the boil, keep covered and simmer very gently for around 2 hours, until the peel can be easily pierced with a knife.

Meanwhile, warm half the sugar in a very low oven. Pour off the cooking water from the oranges into a separate jug and place the oranges on a chopping board. Return the cooking liquid to the pan. Allow the hot oranges to cool until they are easy to handle, then cut them in half, scoop out pips and pith and add these to the reserved orange liquid in the pan. Bring to the boil for around 5 minutes, then strain through a sieve into a bowl. Press the pulp through the sieve with a wooden spoon. This pulp is high in pectin and will help the marmalade set.

Pour half this liquid into a preserving pan. Cut the peel with a sharp knife into fine shreds. Add half the peel to the liquid in the preserving pan with the warm sugar. Stir over a low heat until all the sugar has dissolved, for about 10 minutes, then bring to a rolling boil and allow to cook rapidly for 15- 25 minutes until setting point is reached.

My tried and tested method for finding the perfect setting point is to do the cold plate test: put a small plate in the freezer before you start to make the marmalade. Test for setting point by placing a small drizzle of marmalade on the cold plate. Push it with your finger nail and if it 'wrinkles' then it is at setting point. Test it first after 15 minutes, then again after another few minutes etc, until you can feel that wrinkle is wrinkly enough! Keep the plate in the freezer between tests. Don't overboil the marmalade as it goes tough and crystalises, and you will destroy the lovely colour of the fruit.

Once setting point is reached, cool for five minutes to let the orange peel settle and then pot up into sterilised jars. Careful jar preparation will ensure it remains in perfect condition. We always warm the jars in the oven on a paper lined tray as part of the sterilisation process, and then they are ready for pouring in the marmalade while it is still hot. The steam will push air out through the screwed on lid, creating a good vacuum seal. If you have done this right, you will hear the jar lid 'pop' as the jam cools. Leave to mature for a couple of months before eating.

Make up the other half of the marmalade in exactly the same way.

About the Authors

Yvonne Sonsino

It's probably best to describe me as a bit of a workaholic. I have a day job in the City and help run Ardington in my spare time. I'm also Vice Chair of the Royal Female School of Arts, as well as a practising artist. Plenty of practice still required you might say! I love cooking and entertaining, especially for family, so the baking at Ardington is actually a bit of a treat. I get to bake for hundreds rather than just a few and that's quite something. The recipes are generally quite simple therefore, but you need to use the best ingredients you can find for good flavour. Real butter makes a big taste difference and good flavoured sugars and home-made preserves with home grown produce each bring their own special touch to recipes. I really hope you enjoy some of the secrets shared in this book – the scones and the chocolate cake in particular are long treasured family recipes.

Holly Knight

Holly is our daughter and has worked with Ardington for the past two years, and developed a love of baking after meeting her husband who came back from serving in Afghanistan and missed his home baked treats. Holly says "I was lucky enough to have a Mum and Dad who shared his passion for food and taught me a few tricks along the way. The recipes in this book have bought great joy and happiness to special occasions in my life and I am very honoured to be sharing them with all of the delightful students and tutors who make such an effort to visit the school so regularly. I hope this book brings you a new love of baking and you enjoy it as much as you do the Ardington experience!"

About Ardington School of Crafts

Ardington School of Crafts was founded in 2012 and the current directors - Yvonne & Simon Sonsino - took over in December 2016. They are both passionate about Arts & Crafts and are working hard to develop the curriculum to ensure all tastes and ambitions are covered. There are around 300 workshops arranged each calendar year, delivered by over 60 expert and award winning tutors.

The school is housed in a lovely Victorian school building in the beautiful village of Ardington, South Oxfordshire. The tranquil surroundings and the high quality of tuition provide a creative and relaxed environment. Students often say they feel very welcome and at home here.

Our classrooms are spacious, flooded with natural light and are a pleasure to work in. We have views over grazed farmland and an attractive garden for sunny days. The dining room is a great place to mix with students from other courses and discover shared interests over lunch and at breaks.

In the entrance hall we have a collection of work by our tutors, some of which is also for sale. This collection changes regularly and shows just what you can make on the courses in our packed programme.

We hope you can find time to join us and indulge in the privilege of lifelong learning.

Simon Sonsino
Director and Host at Ardington School of Crafts